The Wit and Wisdom
Barney Stinson

Barney Stinson

For the Bros

Copyright © 2016 Peter Jennings

All rights reserved.

Barnabus "Barney" Stinson is a fictional character created by Carter Bays and Craig Thomas for the CBS television series How I Met Your Mother, portrayed by Neil Patrick Harris. One of the main characters of the show, Barney is a pickup artist who uses a variety of intricate ploys to have meaningless sex with as many women as possible, which is one of the show's central themes. The character is also defined by his love of expensive suits, laser tag, and the catchphrase "Suit up!". In later seasons, however, he matures somewhat, and has a few serious relationships before finally getting married and having a child.

"When I get sad, I stop being sad and be awesome instead."

— Barney Stinson

"A lie is just a great story that someone ruined with the truth."

— Barney Stinson

"Jesus waited three days to come back to life. It was perfect! If he had only waited one day, a lot of people wouldn't have even heard he died. They'd be all, "Hey Jesus, what up?" and Jesus would probably be like, "What up? I died yesterday!" and they'd be all, "Uh, you look pretty alive to me, dude..." and then Jesus would have to explain how he was resurrected, and how it was a miracle, and the dude'd be like "Uhh okay, whatever you say, bro..." And he's not gonna come back on a Saturday. Everybody's busy, doing chores, workin' the loom, trimmin' the beard, NO. He waited the perfect number of days, three. Plus it's Sunday, so everyone's in church already, and they're all in there like "Oh no, Jesus is dead", and then

BAM! He bursts in the back door, runnin' up the aisle, everyone's totally psyched, and FYI, that's when he invented the high five. That's why we wait three days to call a woman, because that's how long Jesus wants us to wait.... True story."

— Barney Stinson

"It's going to be legen...wait for it...and I hope you're not lactose-intolerant cause the second half of that word is...dairy!"

— Barney Stinson

"Suit up!"

— Barney Stinson

"Believe it or not, I was not always as awesome as I am today"

— Barney Stinson

"Article 2: "A Bro is always entitled to do something stupid, as long as the rest of his Bros are all doing it."

― Barney Stinson, The Bro Code

"You know what Marshall needs to do. He needs to stop being sad. When I get sad, I stop being sad, and be awesome instead. True story."

— Barney Stinson

"Ted, I believe you and I met for a reason. It's like the universe was saying, "Hey Barney, there's this dude, he's pretty cool, but it is your job to make him awesome"

— Barney Stinson

"Article 24: "When wearing a baseball cap, a Bro may position the brim at either 12 or 6 o'clock. All other angles are reserved for rappers and the handicapped."

— Barney Stinson, The Bro Code

"Article 100: "When pulling up to a stoplight, a Bro lowers his window so that all might enjoy his music selection."

Corollary: "If there happens to be a hot chick driving the car next to the Bro, the Bro shall put his sunglasses down to get a better look. If he's not wearing his sunglasses, he will first put them on, then pull down to get a better look."

— Barney Stinson, The Bro Code

"Dude... where's your suit? Just once, when I say "suit up" I wish you'd put on a suit."

— Barney Stinson

"Destiny strips at the Melon Patch. They're people Ted, try to keep 'em straight."

— Barney Stinson

"ARTICLE 54 A Bro is required to go out with his Bros on St. Patty's Day and other official Bro holidays, including Halloween, New Year's Eve, and Desperation Day (February 13)."

— Barney Stinson, The Bro Code

"ARTICLE 85 If a Bro buys a new car, he is required to pop the hood when showing it off to his Bros. COROLLARY: His Bros are required to whistle, even if they have no idea what they're whistling at."

— Barney Stinson, The Bro Code

"ARTICLE 41 A Bro never cries. EXCEPTIONS: Watching Field of Dreams, E.T., or a sports legend retire.*"

— Barney Stinson, The Bro Code

"ARTICLE 120 A Bro always calls another Bro by his last name. EXCEPTION: If a Bro's last name is also a racial epithet."

— Barney Stinson, The Bro Code

"ARTICLE 130 If a Bro learns another Bro has been in a traffic accident, he must first ask what type of car he collided with and whether it got totaled before asking if his Bro is okay."

— Barney Stinson, The Bro Code

"Think of me like Yoda, but instead of being little and green I wear suits and I'm awesome. I'm your bro—I'm Broda!"

— Barney Stinson

"Okay, pep talk! You can do this, but to be more accurate, you probably can't. You're way out of practice and she's way too hot for you. So, remember, it's not about scoring. It's about believing you can do it, even though you probably can't. Go get 'em, tiger!"

— Barney Stinson

"In my body, where the shame gland should be, there is a second awesome gland. True story."

— Barney Stinson

"God, it's me, Barney. What up? I know we don't talk much, but I know a lot of girls call out your name because of me."

— Barney Stinson

"Oh right, because there can be too many of something wonderful. Hey Babe Ruth, easy big fella, let's not hit too many homers. Hey Steve Gutenberg, maybe just make three Police Academy movies. America's laughed enough."

— Barney Stinson

"Do you have some puritanical hang up on prostitution? Dude, it's the world's oldest profession."

"Suits are full of joy. They're the sartorial equivalent of a baby's smile."

— Barney Stinson

"Here's the mini-cherry on top of the regular cherry on top of the sundae of awesomeness that is my life."

— Barney Stinson

"Every Halloween, I bring a spare costume, in case I strike out with the hottest girl at the party. That way, I have a second chance to make a first impression."

— Barney Stinson

"You know who is confused? Bimbos. They're easily confused. It's one of the thousand little things I love about them. I love their vacant, trusting stares; their sluggish, unencumbered minds; their unresolved daddy issues. I love them Lily, and they love me. Bimbos have always been there for me, through thick and thin-mostly thin. B-man don't do thick crust, what up!"

— Barney Stinson

"That was the night I was born. I rose like a phoenix from her mentholated bosom and strode into the world, Armani-clad and fully awesome."

— Barney Stinson

"The point is, marriage is stupid. Every day new 22-year olds go into bars, and call me glass-half-full, but I think they're getting dumber."

— Barney Stinson

"This is the time of year when we remember the importance of giving. And there's no greater gift than the gift of booty. So, this holiday season, why not bang someone in need?"

— Barney Stinson

"There are only two reasons to date a girl you've already dated: breast implants."

— Barney Stinson

"See that woman nursing a Black Russian? She's about to chase that with a White American."

— Barney Stinson

"Can't talk my way out of a speeding ticket? I am Barney Stinson, master of manipulation. If I can talk a stripper into paying me for a lap dance, I can talk my way out of a speeding ticket."

— Barney Stinson

"When will you learn that the only difference between my life and porno is my life has better lighting?"

— Barney Stinson

"Trust me when I tell you their universal healthcare system doesn't cover breast implants. If I have to sit through one more flat-chested Nova Scotian riding a Mountie on the back of a Zamboni, I'll go out of my mind."

— Barney Stinson

"Girls are like cartons of milk. Each one has a hotness expiration date and you've hit yours. I'm not saying the occasional guy won't still go to the fridge, open you up, take a sniff, shrug and take a sip anyway: but it's all downhill from here."

— Barney Stinson

"I feel like I've done so much good I have a 'soul boner'."

— Barney Stinson

On Pregnancy Scare

"No part of Barney Stinson does anything less than 110 per cent. If one of my little Michael Phelps' has got loose, he's swimming for a Gold."

— Barney Stinson

"That's what corporate America wants: people who seem like bold risk takers, but never actually do anything."

— Barney Stinson

"This, what you're doing right now? It's giving me a de-rection."

— Barney Stinson

"You are in the heart of Bachelor Country. And as a woman, you are an illegal immigrant here. Now, you could try to apply for a sex visa, but that only lasts 12 hours... 14 if you qualify for multiple entry."

— Barney Stinson

"With great penis comes great responsibility."

— Barney Stinson

"If I could nail any celebrity, it would have to be Scarlett Johansson. She's hot, she's talented, and any woman who does that many Woody Allen movies has to have major daddy issues."

— Barney Stinson

"Can I have your phone number? It's for the bride."

— Barney Stinson

"I only smoke on certain occasions: post-coital, when I'm with Germans - sometimes the two overlap - coital, that time of year the Mets are mathematically eliminated, pre-coital, and – wait for it, 'cause I sure have – pregnancy scares."

— Barney Stinson

"I invest in women who - how can I put this delicately? - they fat! I give them the attention they don't get now, and when they get hot, who do they come to? The guy who gave them attention back when they weren't."

— Barney Stinson

"Soon you will become a henpecked, beaten-down shell of a man. Tonight, we are having a no-holds-barred celebration of brohood; a broing away party; a bro-choice rally; Brotime At The Apollo."

— Barney Stinson

"Open your brain-tank bra, 'cause here comes some premium 91 octane knowledge. There are three rules of cheating: It's not cheating if you're not the one who's married, it's not cheating if her name has two adjacent vowels, and it's not cheating if she's from a different area code. You're fine on all three counts."

— Barney Stinson

Barney: "My, oh, my, there are some ferocious looking cutlets here tonight. OK, hook-up strategy: Find a cutlet, lock her in early, grind with her all night 'till she's mine."

Ted: "Do these strategies ever work for you?"

Barney: "The question is, do these strategies ever not work for me? Either way, the answer's about half the time."

"I am Mr Charity. I frequently sleep with sixes, chubsters and over 30's. I am the Bill and Melinda Gates of the sympathy bang."

— Barney Stinson

"Being single is like a post-apocalyptic wasteland where it's every man for himself. After nine years of captivity, that is my greatest lesson to you."

— Barney Stinson

"You don't bring a date to a wedding. That's like taking a deer carcass on a hunting trip."

— Barney Stinson

"On a booty call, you barely even have to talk. At 9pm you say, 'Hey babe, it's Barney. Are you busy tonight? Sweet, see you in a half an hour.' But the later it gets, the fewer words you need. 12am it's, 'Barney! Busy? Sweet.' And by three in the morning, you just text '?'"

— Barney Stinson

"The rules for dating are the same as the rules for Gremlins. Rule 1: Never get them wet: in other words, don't let her shower at your place. Rule 2: Keep them away from sunlight: ie, never see them during the day. Rule 3: Never feed them after midnight: meaning she doesn't sleep over and you don't have breakfast with her. Ever!"

— Barney Stinson

"There are so many things to do with the human mouth. Why waste it on talking?"

— Barney Stinson

"I'm going out of this world the same way I came into it - buck naked! It's going to be awesome. Open bar for the guys, open casket for the ladies..."

— Barney Stinson

Barney: "Excuse me, did I sleep with you and then screw you over?"

Woman: "No, I don't think so."

Barney: "Dammit! In that case, would you like to go out?"

"There are only three things I would fight: the stubborn clasp of a bra, a paternity suit - nine for 10 - and the urge to vomit whenever I see someone wear brown shoes with a black suit."

— Barney Stinson

"You've been pork free so long, you're practically kosher."

— Barney Stinson

Ted: "The three days rule is stupid. I propose a new rule, the 'You like her, you call her' rule."

Barney: "I'm sorry, I don't speak 'I never get laid'."

"FYI, men don't care. They just want to get to the green, they don't mind going through the rough."

— Barney Stinson

"The camera loves me. More than loves me: the camera lusts me. The camera wants to put on some nice lingerie, pop in an Al Green CD, dim the lights and do me as I lie there with my eyes closed."

— Barney Stinson

Describing the simplicity of running a marathon: "Step one, you start running. There is no step two."

Barney, describing his brother: "He's the awesomest, most best-lookingest, greatest guy ever!"

Lily: "He's exactly like Barney."

Barney: "That's what I just said."

"If there was any shame in a dude getting a pedicure I don't think there would've been a feature about it in Details magazine."

— Barney Stinson

"Now remember my three beginner's tips for picking up chicks: Address her by name, isolate her from her friends, subtly put her down."

— Barney Stinson

"Hello, Ted. If you're watching this tape—and I knew you'd pick this one—you are now in possession of my porn. This can only mean two things: Either I'm dead, or I'm now in a committed relationship. If I'm dead, I want you to honor my memory by taking my body to the Hamptons and re-creating Weekend at Bernie's. I wanna dance, I wanna have sex with a girl, and I wanna go fishing. If, on the other hand, I'm in a committed relationship, then as your best friend, I have only one request: Please, for the love of God, GET ME OUT OF THIS!"

— Barney Stinson

Made in the USA
Middletown, DE
14 September 2024